The Animal Joke Book

Compiled by
Patricia Borlenghi

Illustrated by
Michael Terry

First published in Great Britain in 1998
Bloomsbury Publishing Plc, 38 Soho Square, London, W1V 5DF

A CIP catalogue record of this book is available from the
British Library

ISBN 0 7475 3980 4

Printed in Great Britain by Clays Ltd, St Ives plc

10 9 8 7 6 5 4

This book was compiled with the help of many young people I know. Special thanks to Felix Jakens, who collected the most jokes for me.

But many thanks also to Daniel, Patrick and Leah, Ewan, Katie and Sarah, Georgina, Penny, Mo, Ken and last, but not least, Charlie, Alexander, Lara and Michael.

Some of the jokes are old, some are new and some are plain corny, but we all had great fun collecting them.

This book was compiled with the help of many [illegible] I know. Special thanks to [illegible], who collected the most jokes for me.

Great thanks also to [illegible] and Leah [illegible], Georgina, Penny, [illegible] and last but not least: Charlie, Alexander, Lara and Michaela.

Some of the jokes are old, some are new and some are plain corny, but we all had great fun collecting them.

Contents

What do You Get if You Cross . . .?

What do you get if you cross a sheep with a kangaroo?
A woolly jumper.

What do you get if you cross a baby goat with white chocolate?
The milky baa kid.

What do you get if you cross a bee with a lizard?
A blizzard.

What do you get if you cross a skunk with a boomerang?
A bad smell that keeps coming back.

What do you get if you cross a soldier with a bird?
A parrot-trooper.

What do you get if you cross a cow with a duck?
A cream quacker.

What do you get if you cross a centipede with Ryan Giggs?
A fifty-a-side football match.

What do you get when you cross a chicken with an elephant on Sundays?
A very large roast.

What do you get if you cross a lion with a snowman?
Frostbite.

What do you get when you cross a cobra with a magician?
ABRA DA COBRA.

What do you get if you cross a crocodile with a parrot?
Something that bites your hand off and says: 'Who's a pretty boy, then?'

What do you get if you cross a bear with a skunk?
Winnie the Pooh.

What d'you get if you cross a pig and a dinosaur?
Jurassic Pork.

What would you get if you cross a rodent with a woodpecker?
A rat-a-tat-tat.

What do you get if you cross Dumbo with a ghost?
An elephantom.

What do you get if you cross a hedgehog with a giraffe?
A ten-foot brush.

What do you get if you cross an elephant with a sparrow?
Broken telephone wires.

What do you get if you cross a turkey with a banjo?
A bird that plucks itself.

What do you get if you cross a tortoise with a Golden Retriever?
Something that goes to the shop to get your newspaper and returns two weeks later.

What do you get when you cross a snake with a clown?
Hissterical.

What do you get if you cross a rottweiler with a rose?
Something you wouldn't dare sniff.

What soap opera do you get if you cross a donkey and a bee?
NEIGHBUZZ.

What do you get if you pour boiling water down a rabbit hole?
A hot cross bunny.

What do you get if you run-over a budgerigar with a lawn-mower?
Shredded Tweet!

What's the Difference Between . . .?

What's the difference between a tired dog and a well-dressed man?
One wears suits, the other just pants.

What's the difference between a storm cloud and a man who just sat on a hedgehog?
One pours with rain, and one roars with pain.

What's the difference between a tiny witch and an escaped deer?
One's a stunted hag and the other's a hunted stag.

What's the difference between a fish and a piano?
You can't tuna fish.

What's the difference between a dog and a flea?
A dog can have fleas but a flea can't have dogs.

What's the difference between a weasel and a stoat?
A weasel is weasily recognised and a stoat is stotally different.

What's the difference between an angry football supporter and a cow with a sore throat?
One boos madly and the other moos badly.

Riddles

What do you call a dinosaur with three legs?
A staggersaurus.

What do you call a camel in the North Pole?
Lost.

What do you call a blind deer?
No eye deer.

What do you call a dead, blind deer?
Still no eye deer.

What goes 'croak, croak' when it's misty?
A frog horn.

What goes black white, black white, black white?
A zebra rolling down a hill.

What is black, white and red?
A penguin with sunburn.

What goes ZZUB, ZZUB, ZZUB?
A bee flying backwards.

What's small, furry and sings?
Brian Ferret.

Who plays football in the jungle?
Lion Giggs.

Who solves all the mysteries at the farmyard?
Inspector Horse.

What goes, 'quick, quick.'
A duck with hiccups.

When is the vet busiest?
When it rains cats and dogs.

What's black and yellow and flies underwater?
A bee in a submarine.

What's tall and yellow and smells nice?
A Giraffodil.

What illness did everyone get on the Starship Enterprise?
Chicken spocks.

What's black and white and red on Christmas Eve?
Rudolph the red-nosed penguin.

What's white on the outside and green on the inside?
A frog sandwich.

What's green and goes red at a flick of a switch?
A frog in a blender.

How do you get a milkshake?
Give a cow a pogo-stick.

What has antlers and sucks your blood?
A moose-quito.

What is a grasshopper?
An insect on a pogo stick.

What goes tick tock, bow wow, tick tock, bow wow?
A watch dog.

What goes OOM, OOM.
A cow walking backwards.

What works in a circus, does somersaults and meows?
An acrocat.

What's orange and sounds like a parrot?
A carrot.

What's yellow and dangerous?
Shark-infested custard.

What's yellow and smells of bananas?
Monkey-sick.

What's yellow and nutty?
Squirrel-sick.

What do you call a bear without any ears?
B.

What do you call a dinosaur with one eye?
Doyoureckonhesaurus.

Why are there no asps-in (asprins) the jungle?
Because the parrots-ate -them-all (paracetamol).

Why are fishermen so mean?
Because their job makes them sell-fish.

What is out of bounds?
An exhausted kangaroo.

What's got horns, udders, and cuts grass?
A lawn-moower.

What goes squeak-bang, squeak-bang?
Dynamice.

What's blue and furry?
A mouse holding its breath.

What steals soap from the bathroom?
Robber-ducks.

What has fifty legs but can't walk?
Half a centipede.

What lies on the ground a hundred feet up in the air?
A centipede lying on its back.

How would you catch a perfume thief?
Put a sniffer dog on the scent.

What howls at the moon in frilly knickers?
An underwearwolf.

What's black and red and makes a lot of noise?
A ladybird with a trumpet.

What's black and white, and red on the bottom?
A badger with nappy rash.

What did Rudolph's wife say when a black cloud passed overhead?
'It looks like REIN dear.'

What big, white, lives in the Himalayas and lays eggs?
The abominable snow-chicken.

How do you make a milk shake?
Give a cow a pneumatic drill.

Why are cooks cruel to animals?
They batter fish.

Who has antlers and wears white gloves?
Micky Moose.

What did King Kong say when he found out that his sister had a baby?
'Well, I'll be a monkey's uncle!'

What goes: dot dash, dot dash, neigh?
Horse code.

How does a bird land in an emergency?
By sparrowchute.

What is a caterpillar?
A worm in a fur coat.

What's black and white and bounces?
A penguin on a pogo stick.

Birds, Chickens . . . and

Birds

Why do birds fly south in winter?
Because it's too far to walk?

What do birds watch after the news?
The feather forecast.

What do birds feel like at dinner time?
Peckish.

What do you call a bird that goes Twit-Twoof?
A grrrOWL.

What did the owl do when it had tonsilitis?
It didn't give a hoot.

What numbers sound like an owl when it hoots?
2 – 8 – 2 – 8 -2- 0.

What did the Owl say to his girlfriend when it rained?
Too-wet-to-woo.

What kind of food do Pelicans eat?
Anything that fits the bill.

What do you call someone with a seagull on his head?
Cliff.

At what time do ducks get up in the morning?
At the quack of dawn.

Girl: 'That's not a canary, it's green.'
Second girl: 'Maybe it's not ripe yet.'

Two penguins were arguing about where to go on holiday. One said: ' I know, let's flipper coin to decide.'

'Which bird doesn't build its own nest?'
'A cuckoo.'
'How did you know that?'

'Everyone knows a cuckoo lives in a clock.'

Teacher: 'In the Autumn, birds fly south.'
Boy: 'But sir, if birds fly south why don't worms fly north?'

Woman in petshop.
'Can I have a parrot for my little girl?'
'Sorry, madam, we don't do swops.'

Why does a stork stand on one leg?
Because it would fall over if it lifted the other one.

Teacher: 'If there were five magpies in a tree and the farmer shot one, how many would be left?'
Pupil: 'None, miss, the others would have flown away.'

Chickens

Why did the muddy chicken cross the road twice?
Because he was a dirty double-crosser.

How do you start a cockerel race?
Ready, steady, crow!

How do hens dance?
Chick to chick.

What did the people at Meals-on-Wheels say when they saw a hen?
'Look, eggs on legs!'

What do you call a chicken in a shell suit?
An egg.

Did you hear about the hen who swallowed a yo-yo?
She laid the same egg three times.

What do chickens live in at the North Pole?
An egloo.

Did you hear about the chicken who wanted to take dancing lessons?
She wanted to be a hentertainer.

Crossing the Road . . .

Why did the chicken cross the road?
It saw the zebra crossing.

Why did the crab cross the road?
To get to the other tide.

What did the chicken say to the duck when the chicken didn't want to cross the road?
It's better to be a chicken than a dead duck.

Why did the one-armed monkey cross the road?
To get to the second-hand shop.

Why did the punk cross the road?
It was stapled to the chicken.

Why did the dinosaur cross the road?
Because the chicken hadn't been invented in those days.

Cats . . .

'It was raining cats and dogs yesterday.'
'I know, I stood in a puddle.'

What's worse than raining cats and dogs?
Hailing taxis.

What do cats eat for breakfast?
Mewslie.

How did the cat do in the Milk Race?
He won by six laps.

How do you make a cat flap?
Enter it for Crufts.

What exercise do cats like?
Puss ups.

What do you call a cat that's just eaten a duck?
A duck-filled plattypuss.

What cat discovered America?
Christofurry Colompuss.

What do you call a cat that thinks a lot?
PAWS for thought.

'What's the name of your kitten?'
'I don't know. He won't tell me.'

'Dad, there's a black cat in the kitchen.'
'Black cats are lucky, son.'
'This one is, he's eaten your dinner.'

. . . and Dogs

What do you get if you cross a Rottweiler with Lassie?
A dog who bites your leg off and then runs for help.

Which type of dog hides from frying pans?
A sausage dog.

Which type of dog likes sport?
A Boxer.

How do you stop a dog digging?
Take his spade away!

Why does a dog wag its tail?
Because no-one will wag it for him.

What's a puppy's favourite lesson at school?
Dography.

What dog keeps the best time?
A watch dog.

How do you stop a dog from smelling?
Hold its nose.

Anyone seen the dog bowl?
No, but he makes a great wicket-keeper.

What happened when the man made his dog walk in the gutter?
It fell off the roof.

Why did the dog have its puppies in a dustbin?
On the side it said: 'Place your litter here.'

What is the most famous dog-cricketer?
Graham Pooch.

What's a dog's favourite instrument?
The dinner bell.

Why don't dogs make good dancers?
Because they have two left feet.

What's the main ingredient in dog food?
Collieflower.

Why do bulldogs have flat faces?
Because they chase parked cars!

Where do sick dogs go?
To the dogtors.

Who delivers Christmas presents to dogs?
Santa Paws.

What do you get if you cross a dog with a jeep?
A Land Rover, of course.

What do you call a dog who sits next to a phone?
A Golden Receiver.

'My dog's eaten a camera!'
'Don't worry, nothing will develop.'

What car does a sausage dog drive?
An old banger.

A dog took first prize at a bird show. He ate the prize canary.

Postman to dog owner: ''I have a complaint, your dog bit my ankle.'
Dog owner: 'Well, he's only little – he can't reach your knees.'

Boy to Mum: 'Can I have a puppy for Christmas?'
Mum: 'No, you can have turkey like everyone else!'

Sam: 'Why do you call your dog Camera?'
Alex: 'Because he's always snapping.'

First dog: 'My name's Rover, what's yours?'
Second dog: 'I'm not sure, I think it's Down Boy.'

A hot dog goes into a bar and asks for a drink. The bar attendant says: 'Sorry, we don't serve food in here.'

'That dog bit my leg.'
'Did you put anything on it?'
'No, he liked it just the way it was.'

'Your dog has no tail – how do you know if it's happy?'
'It stops biting me.'

Donkeys and Horses

What do you call a three-legged donkey?
Wonkey.

What do you call a three-legged donkey with one eye?
Winkey-Wonkey.

What do you call a three-legged donkey with B.O.?
Honky-Wonkey.

What did the hungry donkey say when he only had thistles to eat?
'Thistle have to do.'

How do you get five donkeys on a fire-engine?
Two in the front, two in the back and one on the roof going 'ee-aww, ee-aww'.

'Why does he call you donkey?'
'I don't know ee-aww ee-awwlways calls me that.'

Why did the pigeon fly over the race-course?
Because he wanted a flutter on the horses.

What does it mean when you find a horse-shoe?
Some poor horse is walking around in a sock.

What's a horse's favourite game?
Stable Tennis.

Two horses walk into a bar and the barman asks them: 'Why the long faces?'

Elephant Jokes

Elephant in hotel: 'I'm sorry, I can't pay my bill.'
Receptionist: 'Well, you'd better pack your trunk and leave.

What's grey on the inside and pink and white on the outside?
An inside-out elephant.

What is grey and not there?
No elephants.

Why are elephants large, grey and wrinkled?
Because if they were small, white and smooth they'd be aspirins.

Why do elephants wear sandals?
So that their feet don't sink in the sand.

Why do ostriches stick their head in the ground?
To look for the elephants who forgot to wear their sandals.

What was the elephant doing in the telephone box?
He was making a trunk call!

Why do elephants wear small green hats?
So they can sneak across pool tables unobserved.

What did Hannibal say when he saw 1,000 elephants coming over the hill?
'Look, there're 1,000 elephants coming over the hill.'

What did he say when he saw 1,000 elephants with sunglasses on, coming over the hill?
Nothing, he didn't recognise them.

What do you get if you take an elephant into work?
Sole use of the elevator.

What did Tarzan say when he saw the elephants coming over hill?
'Here come the elephants.'

What did he say when he saw the strawberries coming over the hill?
'Here come the elephants.'
He was colour-blind.

'I have to write an essay on an elephant.'
'You'll need a ladder!'

How many elephants can you actually put in a fridge?
Depends on the number of elephants.

Why are there so many elephants running around free in the jungle?
Tarzan's fridge is not large enough to hold them all.

Who lost a herd of elephants?
Big Bo Peep.

What's big and grey and has 16 wheels?
An elephant on roller skates.

How do you know you've got an elephant in your fridge?
It leaves footprints in the butter.

What do you get if you take an elephant into the city?
Free Parking.

How many elephants can you get in a mini?
Two in the front and two in the back.

Why don't elephants like penguins?
They can't get the wrappers off.

What do you call two elephants on a bicycle?
Optimistic!

What day of the week do elephants like best?
Bun-day.

What's big as an elephant and weighs nothing?
An elephant's shadow.

Why shouldn't you go into the woods at 5 o'clock?
Because that's when the elephants do their parachute-jumping.

Why do elephants paint the soles of their feet yellow?
So that they can hide upside-down in bowls of custard.

Did you ever find an elephant in your custard?
No? Well, it must work then.

How do you know there's an elephant under your bed?
Because you need a ladder to get in.

Why are elephants wrinkled?
Have you ever tried to iron one?

What do you get when you cross an elephant with a kangaroo?
Very large holes all over Australia.

How do you know if there is an elephant under the bed?
Your nose is touching the ceiling.

Farmyard

What do you get if you sit under a cow?
A pat on the head!

What do cows read at breakfast?
Moospapers.

Where do cows go for a night out?
To the moo-vies.

Where do cows go on holiday?
Moonorca.

What's a pig's best karate move?
A pork chop.

Two cows standing in a field and one says: 'Mooooooooooo!'
The other says: 'I was just about to say that'.

Two cows talking over a fence. One says to the other: 'Are you worried about this mad cow's disease?' The other says: 'It doesn't bother me, I'm a chicken.'

'In the winter when it's cold my old gran sleeps in the cow shed.'
'What about the smell?'
'Oh, the cows don't mind the smell.'

Why would I buy a cow instead of a bull?
Because I'd get free milk from a cow, but a bull would charge.

How do sick pigs get to hospital?
Easy, in a hambulance.

What's a pig's favourite football player?
Ryan Pigs.

What do you put on a pig with a bruise?
Oink-ment.

Did you know it takes more than 10 sheep to make one sweater?
I didn't know sheep could knit.

Which farm animal talks too much?
Bla bla black sheep.

How do you count cows?
With a cow-culator.

Why did the cow go to the North Pole?
To get some calpol.

Why do cows lie down in the rain?
To keep each udder dry.

What's ten feet tall and smelly?
A pig on stilts.

Fish and Other Sea Creatures

Did you hear about the deaf fish?
He wore a herring-aid.

What do you call a fish that swims in and out of goal posts?
A goalkipper.

How do you make an octopus laugh?
Give it ten tickles.

Why was the crab arrested?
Because it kept pinching things.

What kind of noise annoys an oyster?
A noisy noise annoys an oyster.

What do you get from an educated oyster?
Pearls of wisdom.

What do you get if you cross an owl with an oyster?
A bird that drops pearls of wisdom.

What fish sleep a lot?
Kippers!

Why is a fish shop always crowded?
Because the fish fill-et.

A dolphin bumps into another dolphin, and said: ' I didn't do it on porpoise!'

Which fish wears a cowboy hat and has two guns?
Billy the Squid.

What do you get from a hungry shark?
As far away as possible.

Why wouldn't the shark eat my sister?
Because it was a man-eater.

How do you get two Whales (to Wales) in a mini?
Down the M4 and across the Severn Bridge.

If a whale had a boy and girl twins they would be blubber and sister.

What do whales eat?
Fish and ships.

'Does your house suffer from damp?'
'I'll say, I found a fish in the mousetrap the other day.'

'Sorry son, but you need a permit to fish here.'
'Thanks all the same, but I'm doing quite well with a worm.'

'I keep my pet goldfish in the bath.'
'What do you do when you want a bath?'
'Blindfold them.'

A man comes in with a fish. 'Look what I came home with. I could be a fisherman!'
Boy says, 'I came home with a pint of milk. Will I become a cow?'

Tramp: 'Typical, when I want old boots, all I get is fish!'

Why couldn't the fish sing in the girls' choir?
It was a bass.

Gorillas, etc.

Where does a forty-stone gorilla sit in a cinema?
Anywhere it likes.

What do you call a gorilla with a banana in each ear?
Anything you like.

What do you call a monkey who loves chips?
A chip-monk!

Why is it easy for monkeys to make a song?
Because they can swing a tune.

How does a monkey make toast?
He puts it under a G(O)RILLA.

Where do baby apes sleep?
In an apricot.

What d'you call a baboon with a Kalashnikov?
Sir.

What kind of ape talks a lot?
A Blaboon.

Hedgehogs

Why did the hedgehog say 'ouch, ouch, ouch?'
Because he put his coat on inside out.

Why did the hedgehog cross the road?
To prove he had guts.

Why did the hedgehog cross the road?
To see his flat mate.

What do hedgehogs eat for lunch?
Prickled onions.

Did you hear about the short-sighted hedgehog? – He fell in love with a pin-cushion.

How do hedgehogs play leapfrog?
Very carefully.

A hedgehog was crossing the road and he heard a car coming so he thought:

'If I get to the middle of the road the car won't squash me'. So he crawled into the middle of the road. But somehow the car ran him over. How did this happen?

The car was a Robin Reliant.

Insects

What do you call a musical insect?
A humbug.

How do you make a butterfly?
Get a fly and spread butter on it.

Why didn't the spider feel well?
Because it caught a nasty bug.

What do you call an Irish spider?
Paddy Longlegs.

What do girl spiders wear when they get married?
Webbing dresses.

Where do giant spiders play soccer?
At Webley Stadium.

Spider: 'I've just had a nasty shock. There's a big hairy man in the bath.'

Why do bees hum?
Because they don't know the words.

What did the bee say to the flower?
Hi, honey!

How do bees get from place to place?
By buzz.

Why do bees have sticky hair?
Because they use honeycombs.

Knock, knock.
Who's there?
Bumble bee.
Bumble bee cold if you don't wear pants.

What never shows off about being able to make honey?
A humble bee.

What do you call a deaf wasp?
Anything you want.

Where do you take injured wasps?
To the waspital.

Why did the fly do an old-fashioned dance on the jam jar?
Because it said: 'Twist to open.'

What's the last thing that goes through a fly when its hits a car windscreen?
Its bottom.

How d'you keep flies out of your kitchen?
Put a bucket of manure in your sitting-room.

'Waiter, what's this fly doing in my soup?'
'Looks like the breast-stroke.'

What time is it when a flea and a fly pass each other?
Fly past flea.

Why did the flea lose its job?
It wasn't up to scratch.

How do you start a flea race?
One-two-flea-go!

What did the mother-worm say to the little worm who was late?
'Where in earth have you been?'

What are the largest ants in the world?
Eleph-ants.

What do you call someone who buys and sells insects?
An ant-tic dealer.

What did the cricket say to his mate when they had an argument?
'You hypocrick.'

What do you call a spider with no legs?
A currant!

Why did the ant run across the top of the cereal packet?
Because it said tear across the dotted line!

Kangaroos

What do you do to a kangaroo with appendicitis?
Hoperate on him.

Why did the kangaroo scold her baby?
For eating biscuits in bed.

Name three animals you would find in Australia?
Er . . . a kangaroo and two sheep.

How do you stop a kangaroo race?
Tie the kangaroo down, sport, tie the kangaroo down.

Rhymes

There was a young man from Leek
Who instead of a nose had a beak.
It grew quite absurd
Till he looked like a bird.
He migrates at the end of next week.

Little boy blue, come blow your horn.
The sheep's in the meadow, the cow's in the corn.
But where is the boy who looks after the sheep?
He's stuck in the quicksand, fifty feet deep.

There was a young boy called Dale,
who wanted to eat a whole whale.
He mashed it with cheese
and served it with peas,
but couldn't quite manage the tail.

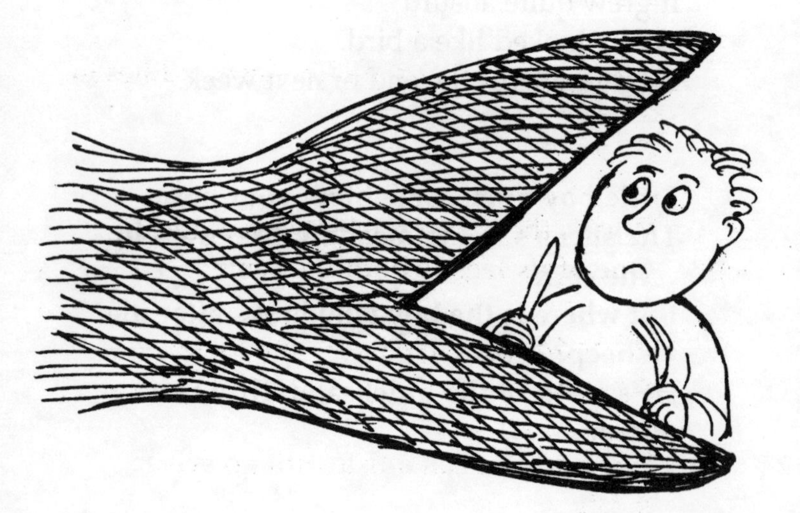

Surreal

How many surrealists does it take to change a light-bulb?
Fish.

What's green, has a million legs and lies in a field?
Grass.

What's the difference between a duck?
One of its legs is both the same.

What do you call a fly with no wings?
A walk.

What do you call a fish with no eyes?
A fsh.

What do you call a sheep with no legs?
A cloud.

What's got four wheels and flies?
A dustcart.

Why did the koala bear fall out of the tree?
Because it was dead.

Why did the second koala bear fall out of the tree?
It was holding hands with the first one.

Why did the third koala bear fall out of the tree?
It thought it was a game.

Shaggy Dog Types . . .

Two sheep in a field. The first sheep says: 'Moo, moo.'

The second sheep asks: 'Sorry, but what are you saying?'

The first sheep says: 'I'm learning a new language.'

A boy walks into a petshop and asks to buy a wasp.

'We don't sell wasps', says the petshop owner.

'Yes, you do,' says the boy, ' there are two in the window.'

An explorer is travelling through the jungle and he comes across a dead lion. Standing by the dead lion is a pygmy.

'Did you kill this lion?' asked the explorer.

'Yes,' said the pygmy.

'Sorry to ask, but HOW?'

'With my club.'

'It must be a very big club.'

'Yes, there are 30 of us in it.'

A mother polar bear and a baby polar bear are sitting on an ice floe in the North Pole.

'Mum, am I really a polar bear?'

'Yes dear ,' she says.

Five minutes later: 'Are you sure I'm a polar bear?'

'Yes dear, of course you are. I'm a polar bear, your father's a polar bear, and you are a polar bear.'

Another five minutes passes: 'Are you really, really sure I'm a polar bear.'

'Look, darling,' his mother replies, rather annoyed now, 'you are definitely a polar bear – please be quiet now, I'm trying to fish.'

Another five minutes passes: 'Are you really, really, really sure I'm a polar bear.'

Mother is now really angry: 'How many more times? You are definitely a polar bear! What is the matter with you?'

Baby looks up rather pathetically and says: 'I'm flipping freezing!'

The Lion thinks he's the King of the Jungle. He's walking round the jungle and sees some monkeys. He asked the monkeys if he's the king of the jungle. 'Yes, you are, oh mighty one,' they reply.

He then meets some gazelles and asks them the same question. 'Yes, you are, oh mighty one,' they reply.

Then he meets an elephant and asks him the same question. The elephant picks him up and swings him round and throws him down on the ground.

'Just because he didn't know the answer!' sighs the lion.

A man is walking down the road with a penguin. A policeman notices them and says to the man: 'Take that penguin to the zoo immediately!'

The man says, 'OK', and off he goes with the animal.

The next day, the policeman sees the same man walking along with the penguin.

'I thought I told you to take that penguin to the zoo!' shouts the officer.

The man replies, 'I did, and he liked it so much that today I'm taking him to the cinema.'

A plumber arrives at Mr and Mrs Smith's to repair a leak. But Mr & Mrs Smith have gone out for the day, forgetting the plumber is coming. The plumber knocks on the front door, little realising that the Smiths' parrot can hear everything.

'Who's that?' a shrill voice squeaks.

'It's the plumber' – comes the reply.

'Who's that?' a shrill voice squeaks again.

'It's the plumber' – comes the reply once again.

'Who's that?' the shrill voice squawks again.

'It's THE PLUMBER,' replies the plumber loudly.

And again the voice chirps: 'Who's that?'

The plumber replies and replies, louder and louder, until at the umpteenth 'Who's that?' he collapses exhausted in a heap by the front door.

Mr and Mrs Smith return, and see the man on the front door step, and Mrs Smith asks her husband, 'George, who's that?' A voice squeaks from behind the front door: 'It's the plumber!'

Aboard a cruise ship, some entertainers prepare for the evening. The captain has a very clever parrot which watches everyone. The parrot is fascinated by the magician and his tricks and he loves telling the crowd how the tricks are done.

This gets on the magician's nerves, but he gets on with his job patiently and quietly shuffles the cards. He offers the pack to someone in the audience, 'Take a card sir.'

The man takes a card and the magician puts it back in the pack.

'It's up his sleeve,' squawks the bird.

The poor magician knows his trick is ruined.

The magician produces a rabbit from his top hat. The same thing happens again.

'It's in his jacket,' squawks the parrot.

The magician tries to saw a lady in half.

'There's a mirror,' shouts the parrot.

Every evening the same thing happens, and the magician is getting very fed up.

One night, during the magician's act, the sea gets really rough and the ship strikes a rock and in no time the ship sinks, leaving people floundering around in the water.

The magician makes it to the lifeboat, and a minute later, the parrot also reaches the lifeboat. The parrot sits on the edge of the life-raft staring at the magician for ages, until finally it pipes up and says:

'All right wise guy, what did you do with the ship?'

A snail goes into a bar on New Year's Eve and asks for a drink.

The bartender says: 'We don't serve snails in here.'

The snail says: 'Oh come on, here's the money.'

The bartender says: 'I've told you, we don't serve snails.'

The snails says: 'Oh come on, I've got the right money.'

The bartender says: 'I'm getting annoyed with you now, I can't serve you.'

The snail says: ' Oh come on, it's New Year's Eve.'

The bartender says: 'Right, that's it, I'm going to throw you out now.' And he throws the snail out of the door.

Next New Year's Eve the same snail goes into the bar and asks the bartender: 'What did you do that for?'

A young man has had a hard day at work, so on his way home he thinks he will cheer himself up by buying a takeaway curry – a nice spicy Chicken Vindaloo.

When he gets home he gets himself a drink, puts the curry on a plate on the table in front of the television. He is just about to sit down when the phone rings. He goes to answer it in the hallway, and when he gets back the cat is sitting on the table eating the curry.

'Right,' he says to the cat, 'you've had it!' He grabs the cat, takes it outside to the garden, and shoves it in the water butt. He raids the fridge for some bread and cheese, and then sits down and watches the TV, feeling really fed up.

Ten minutes later, there is a knock at the back door. He answers it and the cat is standing there and it says:

'Have you got any more water, please?'

A woman goes into a shop with a giraffe and the giraffe lies down on the floor.

The shopkeeper says to the woman: 'You can't leave that lying there.' And the woman says: 'It's not a lion, it's a giraffe.'

A man goes into the butcher's and asks for an ox tail.

So the butcher says: 'Well, once upon a time there was this cow . . .'

A Polar Bear walks into a bar and says:

'. . . Um, um . . . can I have . . . um, um . . . an . . . um, um . . . coke, please?'

And the bartender says: 'Why the long paws, then?'

A woman and her dog walk to the bus-stop.

There's a man already at the bus-stop eating a big meat pie.

He says to the woman: 'Would you like me to throw your dog a bit?'

She says: 'Oh, that's very nice of you – yes please!'

So the man picks up the dog and throws it across the road.

There was once a squid that escaped from an aquarium in Brighton. It went into the English Channel and swam a little way out. Now, this squid was not used to the cold water as he had lived in the warm waters of the aquarium. A shark came along and said:

'What's the matter with you then?'

And the squid answered: 'I'm really cold, and I feel positively sick.'

'I'll carry you back to where you belong then,' said the shark. So the squid jumped on the shark's back and the shark started to carry the squid. They travelled hundreds of miles and the water kept getting warmer and warmer, but the squid was still very sick. Then the shark saw some of his friends and flicked the squid off in their direction, and said to his friends: 'Here's that six quid I owe you.'

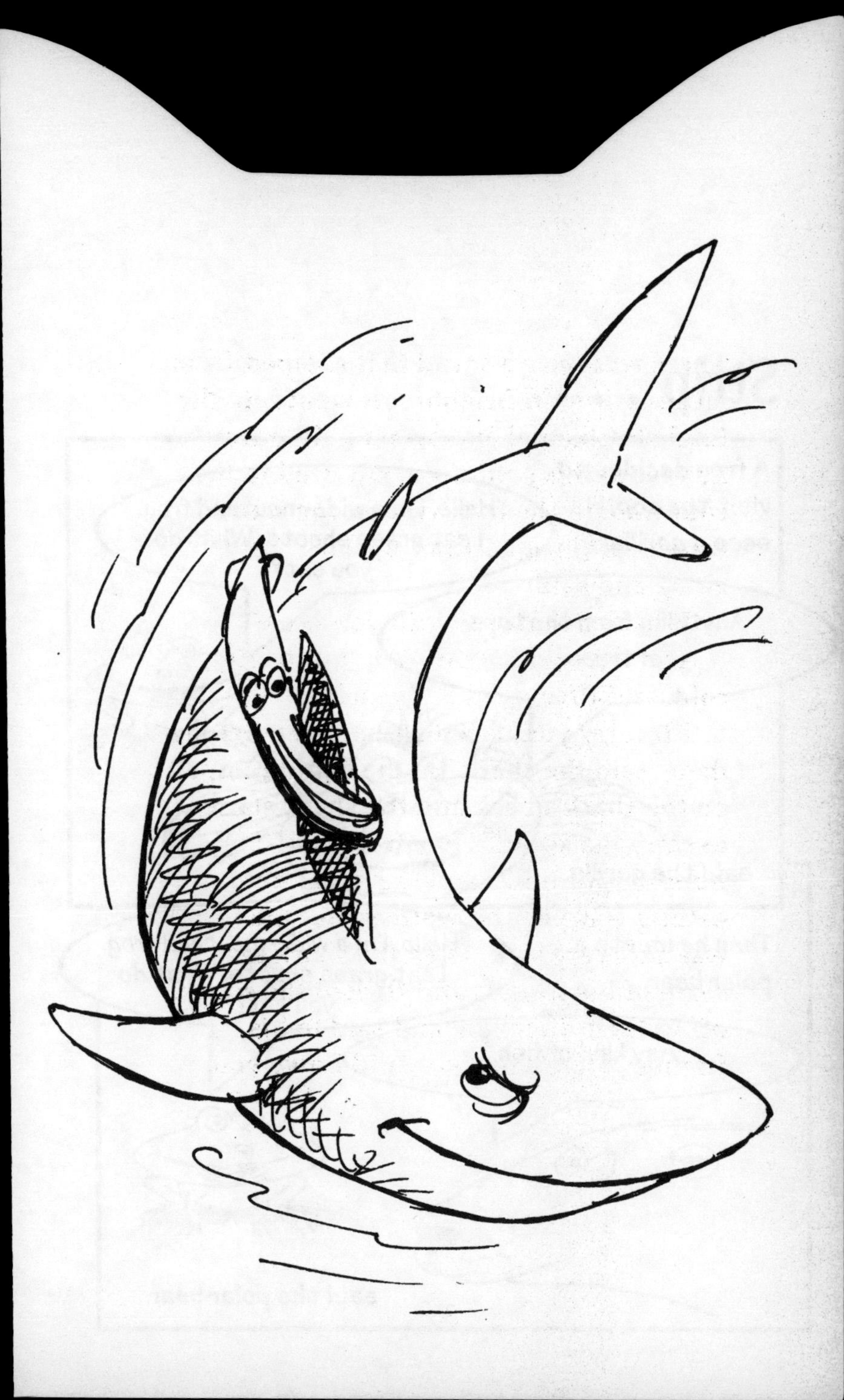

Strip . . .

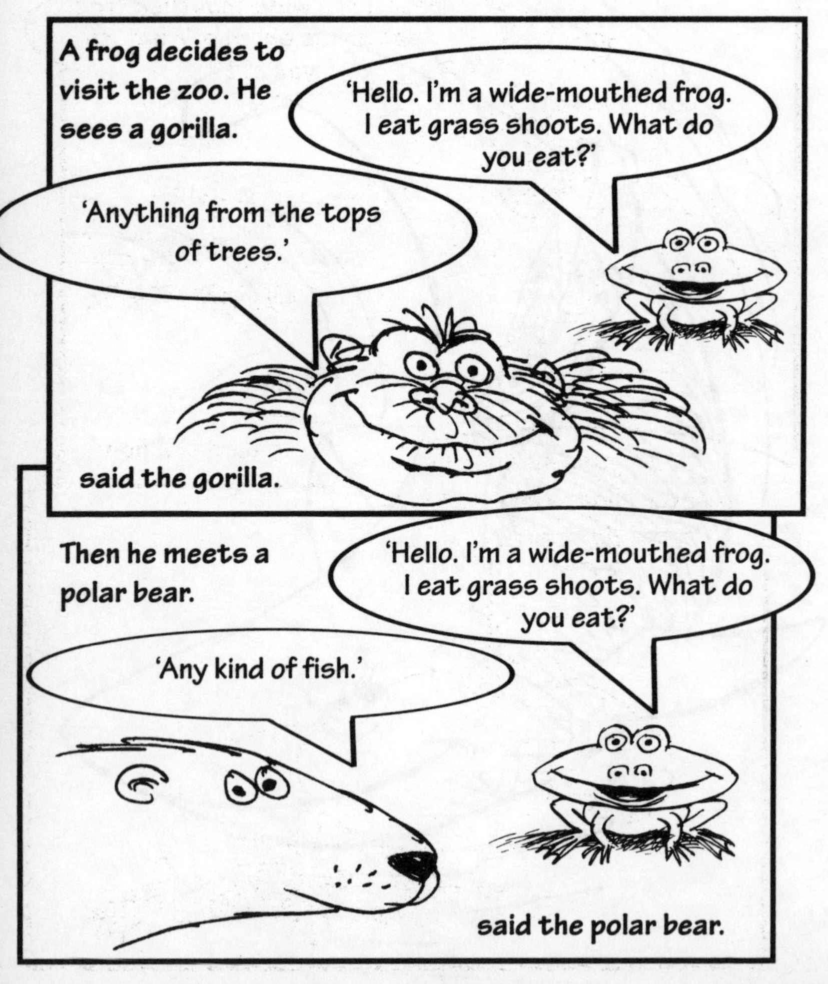
A frog decides to visit the zoo. He sees a gorilla.
'Hello. I'm a wide-mouthed frog. I eat grass shoots. What do you eat?'
'Anything from the tops of trees.'
said the gorilla.
Then he meets a polar bear.
'Hello. I'm a wide-mouthed frog. I eat grass shoots. What do you eat?'
'Any kind of fish.'
said the polar bear.

Then he meets a lion.
'Hello. I'm a wide-mouthed frog. I eat grass shoots. What do you eat?'
'Wide-mouthed frogs.'
said the lion.
'Oooh, yoou doon't see many of thoose aroond here, do yoou?'

Two frogs having a conversation:

Tail-Enders . . .

What steals soap from the bathroom?
An animal that barks at submarines.

Where do animals sell their old junk?
At a jungle sale.

How many skunks does it take to clear a tramp out of a house?
Quite a PHEW!

What do skunks have that no other animals have?
Baby skunks.

Where do you find hippos?
Depends where you left them.

What is a furry alligator?
A bear that went into the woods at 5 o'clock.

'Waiter, can I have an alligator sandwich? And make it snappy.'

'There's a man at the door with a bill!'
'That's not a man, it's a duck!'

What did the two boa-constrictors do when they fell in love?
They had a crush on each other.

Why does no-one play cards in the jungle?
Because there are too many Cheetas.

What did the father buffalo say to his youngster when he went to school?
'BI SON.'

Did you hear about the two deer who ran away to get married? They antELOPED.

Why can't you have a conversation with a goat around?
Because it keeps butting in.

What kind of sweets do frogs like?
Lolli-hops.

What kind of lights did Noah and his animals have on the Ark?
Floodlights.

Why are giraffes' necks so long?
Because they can't stand the smell of their feet.

How do you catch a squirrel?
Climb up a tree and act like a nut.

What's a zebra?
A horse too lazy to take off his pyjamas.

What did the baby mouse say when it first saw a bat?
'Look, mum, an angel!'

What fruit do vampire bats like best?
Blood oranges and NECK-tarines.

Why do you never kiss a vampire?
Because they have bat breath.

Why do the French eat snails?
Because they don't like fast food.

What's the best thing to do if you find two snails fighting?
Let them slug it out.

When is a man-eating tiger likely to enter the house?
When the door is open.

Why is a dragon the best kisser?
Because he has hot lips.

What do you call an aardvark who keeps getting beaten up?
A vark, cos he's not ard any more.

A young aardvark is harmless.
Why is that?
Because a little aardvark never hurt anybody.

Boy: 'I'm sorry I'm late, sir, there was a lion in my garden.'
Teacher: 'How scary, poor boy!'
Boy: 'Not really, sir, it was a dandelion.'

Two snails robbed a tortoise.
'Can you describe the thieves?'
'No, it all happened so quickly.'

Teacher: 'Henry VII, Henry VIII, Mary. Who came after Mary?'
Pupil: ' Er, . . . her little lamb?'

Zebra talking to his mum:
'Mum, why can't I have an Arsenal shirt?'
Mrs Zebra: 'It's too expensive, you'll have to support Newcastle United like the rest of us.'